CONOZCO LAS ESTACIONES DEL AÑO
I KNOW THE SEASONS

By Jon Welzen
Traducido por Fátima Rateb

Gareth Stevens
PUBLISHING

conceptos básicos

Conozco las cuatro
estaciones.

I know the four seasons.

Las cuatro estaciones son invierno, primavera, verano y otoño.

The four seasons are winter, spring, summer, and fall.

invierno/winter

primavera/spring

verano/summer

otoño/fall

5

El invierno es frío.

Winter is cold.

Veo nieve en invierno.

I see snow in winter.

9

La primavera es lluviosa.

Spring is rainy.

11

Veo nuevas plantas
en primavera.

I see new plants
in spring.

13

El verano es caluroso.

Summer is hot.

15

Nado en verano.

- -

I swim in summer.

17

El otoño es fresco.

Fall is cool.

19

Veo hojas de muchos
colores en otoño.

I see many colors
of leaves in fall.

21

¿Qué estación
te gusta más?

What season
do you like best?

23

Please visit our website, www.garethstevens.com. For a free color catalog of all our high-quality books, call toll free 1-800-542-2595 or fax 1-877-542-2596.

Cataloging-in-Publication Data

Names: Welzen, Jon.
Title: I know the seasons = Conozco las estaciones del año / Jon Welzen.
Description: New York : Gareth Stevens Publishing, 2017. | Series: What I know = Lo que conozco | In English and Spanish
Identifiers: ISBN 9781482462074 (library bound)
Subjects: LCSH: Seasons–Juvenile literature.
Classification: LCC QB637.4 W45 2017 | DDC 508.2–dc23

First Edition

Published in 2017 by
Gareth Stevens Publishing
111 East 14th Street, Suite 349
New York, NY 10003

Translator: Fátima Rateb
Editorial Director, Spanish: Nathalie Beullens-Maoui
Editor, English: Therese Shea
Designer: Sarah Liddell

Photo credits: Cover, p. 1 (stripes) Eky Studio/Shutterstock.com; cover, p. 1 (seasons) Piotr Krzeslak/Shutterstock.com; p. 3 pavelgr/Shutterstock.com; p. 5 Ingrid Prats/Shutterstock.com; p. 7 Pressmaster/Shutterstock.com; p. 9 Kotenko Oleksandr/Shutterstock.com; p. 11 wanphen chawarung/Shutterstock.com; p. 13 Sofiawood/Shutterstock.com; p. 15 loskutnikov/Shutterstock.com; p. 17 Tom Wang/Shutterstock.com; p. 19 Jacek Chabraszewski/Shutterstock.com; p. 21 Anna Moskvina/Shutterstock.com; p. 23 GoodMood Photo/Shutterstock.com.

Printed in the United States of America

CPSIA compliance information: Batch #CW17GS: For further information contact Gareth Stevens, New York, New York at 1-800-542-2595.